The Broken Bowl
(New and Uncollected Poems)

by

James A. Emanuel

Lotus Press
Detroit
1983

International Standard Book Number: 0-916418-42-1
Library of Congress Catalogue Number: 82-083858

Printed in the United States of America

Lotus Press, Inc.
Post Office Box 21607
Detroit, Michigan 48221

To the memory of
MY SON, JAMES,
who in his purest light
will long outlive
three cowardly cops
in San Diego

Other books of poetry by James A. Emanuel:

The Treehouse and Other Poems (1968)
Panther Man (1970)
Black Man Abroad: The Toulouse Poems (1978)
A Chisel in the Dark (Poems: Selected and New) (1980)
A Poet's Mind (1983)

Contents

Preface

The Broken Bowl was fashioned as the kind of book that apparently does not exist in the Black American tradition — the kind, however, that is indispensable if the lifework of any poet is to be conveniently available for assessment. There is no need to scour the pages of periodical indexes and bibliographies, and then search newspapers and journals, to discover the uncollected works that living poets can handily provide. There is no need to conjecture — and no excuse for ignoring — the period when a poem was composed or the date when it was first published if the foremost authority on these matters can have the data printed with the poem itself.

My inclusion in *The Broken Bowl* of uncollected early pieces, together with their dates of composition at the bottom left and their dates of first publication at the bottom right, is not meant to attribute any particular quality to the poems or any certain pattern in their evolution. That practice, however, enables the reader to verify such predictable minor facts as the period when *Black* replaced *Negro* in my work; also it allows him (if he examines my previous books of poetry and the volume of selected works that I hope to publish) to determine such unguessable major facts as the beginning of my almost total exclusion of rime, or the chronological pattern of my concern for love, or — if aided by my autobiographical *Snowflakes and Steel* — the temporal explanations of my recurrent treatments, after 1968, of personal and racial injustice.

More important is the possibility that other Black poets will begin to assemble the best of their uncollected publications and date them with a similar system — to be preserved as method in the authors' ultimate "selected works" — to remind readers that literary history is nourished by small facts that signal large meanings to be reached for, long trails to be followed. Black poets (and presses) thus can now outreach those traditional publishers of anthologies who in omitting such information have remained simply bookmakers, and can outdistance those warring Black critics who in the 1970's were image-makers: they can become, in the 1980's, history-makers, new in their seriously disciplined vision of the future.

That vision, if institutionalized, might lead to some pioneering service, some Black repository into which generations of academic "groupies" could dip repeatedly: some place of national storage where poets would be invited to send copies of their published but uncollected works for scholarly study — an ebony bowl to hold the treasures for which we poets dig into ourselves.

The many years between "Primavera" and "Racism in France" are awesome enough as a number. They are more awesome still as a poetic life to be measured along its skyline rather than its underbrush. Imponderably, they cannot guarantee that the quality of any one of the twenty-nine new poems, written in France, England, Sweden, Switzerland, Romania, and Bulgaria, will touch more horizon than shrubbery.

But awe and sky are enough to keep going on.

J.A.E.
10 May 1983

Primavera

No bills laud Primavera.
The herald of her show
May be the softness of the ground,
The way the breezes blow.

The stage may be a longing
For romance yet unseen,
Or eager hope in youthful eyes
Upon a leaf turned green.

The winds of March give prelude,
And the curtain is drawn high
On the wings of the first robin
Till it blends in with the sky.

With her head bowed in a flower,
Primavera hears it sing,
And, rising, brings to us again
The grand ballet of Spring.

1946   *1946*

Tomorrow

This day makes sport of my desire,
And laughter echoes my lament.
My joy is ransomed by tomorrow,
To whose embrace my toil is bent.

Tomorrow will descend a queen
From this day's own pure atmosphere,
Diademmed and royal gowned,
Steadfastly throned without compeer.

Her sweeping grace shall light on me,
The cherished in her loving sway;
And sweet release shall find, at morn,
This luckless duel I wage today.

Today is borne on fledgling wings
Weakened where my eyes can see;
Tomorrow rides with eagles strong
Whose flight points to eternity.

1947   *1947*

Gone

I came back and found you gone . . .
Where I came back, I do not know,
And when, I cannot tell.
There is no time without you,
Nor place, if it does not echo
To your laughter.

You have taken my sanity with you.
I looked for you in the closet, in impossible places.
I asked a little child if he had seen you pass,
And peered into the faces of strange women.
I have searched all the places I have taken you
And places I saw you before you knew my name.

Even as I look for you I know you mean
To be found – by another – as I found you,
With a lullaby for a lonely heart.
You will tease his sorrow into desire and on
To melancholy. And then one day
He will come back and find you gone . . . .

1949   *1949*

Sonnet for a Writer

Far rather would I search my chaff for grain
And cease at last with hunger in my soul,
Than suck the polished wheat another brain
Refurbished till it shone, by art's control.
To stray across my own mind's half-hewn stone
And chisel in the dark, in hopes to cast
A fragment of our common self, my own,
Excels the mimicry of sages past.
Go forth, my soul, in painful, lonely flight,
Even if no higher than the earthbound tree,
And feel suffusion with more glorious light,
Nor envy eagles their proud brilliancy.
Far better to create one living line
Than learn a hundred sunk in fame's recline.

1953   *1958*

The Circuit of Despair

I went mining into darkness,
Seeking pits of blacker night,
Tunneling ahead of terror,
Fleeing from a ray of light.

Faster flew my feet descending,
Strong my arms to break the way,
Closing lids on stars behind me,
Blinking back the threat of day.

Deep inside the realm of silence,
Nestling, curling, tranquil now,
I drank sweetly of the ether
That the lowest stones allow.

But the lowest stone of all,
With its structure hard and neat,
Stamped a perfect word of wonder
On my brow and on my feet.

I went mining up through darkness.
Strong my arms to break the way.
I drank sweetly of the ether
Lighting with the word the day.

(ca. 1958)   *1959*

A Fable for Animals

The driver's cursemouth spat with his whip's slow crack,
And the one-ton mare, the monster roan, ears back,
Lunged belly-low uphill to stir each wheel
The mud sucked down. In vain. More goaded zeal,
More beast-brawn poured its dumb, obedient heart
Into the leathered chains. They snapped apart.
The team reared high, inhaled lost power that broke
Like lightning through the links and shook the yoke.

In deadly pause, the beast-world turned to gaze:
Although the bland-eyed cow did only raise
And twitch her head, the killdeer dipped his wing;
The rattlesnake spiralled from a windrow string.
Thrilled, far away, the Beast of the sleepless eyes
Burned at the straining yoke. Iron ribs that rise
Like lava round a hot-core heart inhaled . . . .
He sped, well followed, toward the bonds that failed.

(ca. 1960)   *1962*

16

When I Read of the Rose of Dachau
(*New York Post*, **March 23, 1960**)

Auschwitz!
Buchenwald!
Smart makers of the dead,
Enjoy
This Rose of Dachau.

Whore,
Ever scarlet.

Bitter-strange
I knew you not
In my bride's bright hand
Or by my wearied mother's
Stone-pressed brow.

Lovely witch,
Hold your beauty
Still.

Or is it I,
Or is it I
Who tremble?

1960   *1962*

Note: *The newspaper reported that roses had been thickly planted over the sites of atrocities at the concentration camp at Dachau.*

It Was a Happy Little Grave

It was a happy little grave:
Cool silken sand the mound,
The sugar loaf that browned her throat
And pressed her curls aground.

Some bathers on the jocund beach
In silence eyed the frame
A boy heaped on his sister's smiles,
To make of death a game.

The mother shook a bright curl free;
Her glance forbade the spade,
And casually caressed the hand
That wrecked what it had made.

It was a happy little grave
For squeals to occupy —
Now just sand beneath the feet
Of noisy passers-by.

(ca. 1962)   *1963*

Eichmann, Slide No. 6

My eye to the glass,
I breathed on his sneer.
I polished the lens,
But the mist did not clear.

(ca. 1962)   *1963*

A Pause for a Fine Phrase

I meditate right off the page.
Quick memory and pleasing rage
And soothing slide of conscious mind
Move to the brink, and there I find
A meaning more than what you meant
Gleaming in a corner bent
Right out of flooring that you laid
For stud and joist you never made.
The corner turns and comes to me,
Then something fits, and I am free
To lift my finger off the line
That you have made completely mine.

(ca. 1962)   *1963*

Beyond the Clearing

The patient animals are standing by.
The scythe-beaked eagles, villain mountaineers,
Have clutched in silver claws our only spears;
The olive branch they wrenched has withered dry.
The Scorpion more darkly blots our sky
And deepens his cave when autumn sun appears.
Gargoyles that pulled our boats through pagan meres
Now puke on our streets and blankly prophesy.
Two chimpanzees have dared for us the moon;
Three grounded monkeys teach us to be wise:
That dumb-and-blind-and-deaf will keep in tune.
And in the schoolyard loud with children's cries
Two lions sit in stone, bereft of noon,
To watch and wait, with granite in their eyes.

(ca. 1963)   *1963*

For a Farmer

Something slow moves through him, watched by hills.
Something low within each rock receives
His noonday wish, then crumbles rich; so fills
Each furrow that the prairie year upheaves.
His arm has lain with boulders. His copper hand
Has mused on roots, uncaring of barbed wire.
His fist has closed on thistle, and dug the land
For corn October snows have whelmed entire.
Something flows with him in stubborn streams,
And in the parted foliage something lives
In upright green, stirred by the rhythmic gleams
Of his hoe and spade. From worn-out arms he gives;
The earth receives, turns all his pain to soil,
Where he believes, and testifies through toil.

(ca. 1963)   *1964*

Whatever Broken Thing You Have

Whatever broken thing you have is past.
Let go, set free the fragments of design
We cannot know. The pieces cannot last.
Our little gasp of pain cannot align
What is to be with what is done. Somewhere
All splinters fit, except the one we keep.
All craft adrift do float toward some care
Or bubble cleanly down into the deep.
One great design awaits. The island shifts,
The sea remains, and all that seems to drown
With unrecorded navies lulls and lifts
A treasure world, and wears a weedless crown.
Cut loose, cast off, fear nothing at the bar:
The shore will turn and come to where you are.

(ca. 1963)   *1964*

Sarah at the Sink

She scrubs for something more than clean.
Her hands need more than what hands mean.
Porcelain as bright as snow
Has not the place she wants to go.
Suds immaculately hop
Around the hands that cannot stop.
Elbow-pistons smartly pound,
But all is quiet: just the sound
Of acrobatic bubbles swirled
Around a briefly shining world.

1963   *1964*

24

Effigy

Button-eyed bastard
Of kicked-up straw,
Uncrying body,
Burlap jaw,
Swing
For their upturned faces.

Wrenchbellied
Twist of spite,
Knotted core
Where godlike right
To shape was fouled,
Writhe
For their upturned faces.

Effigy,
Stitchmouthed rag spittoon,
Shoulders limp
Against the moon,
Bleed
For their upturned faces.

(ca. 1963)   *1964*

Black Muslim Boy in a Hospital

Are you hot there too?
(Down in the grates of you,
Banked for long burning,
Some cindered yearning,
Locked in despair,
Kindles your glare.)

Does it hurt? (Something cries
When I gently press your eyes.
A tiny light in you goes out,
Blinking in a stream of doubt,
When this white though healing hand
Trespasses and takes command.)

(Hate for friends and hate for foes
Who have not endured hate's blows
Digested with the crumbs of years.
What can stop these ancient tears
Burning in a little face
So captive in a starched embrace?)

(ca. 1963)   *1964*

A Fool for Evergreen

A little bit of fool in me
Hides behind my inmost tree
And pops into the narrow path
I walk blindfolded by my wrath
Or shrunken by some twist of pain,
Some hope that will not wind again.
He ogles with his antic eyes
And somersaults a you're-not-wise
Until the patches in his pants
Go colorwheeling through my glance
So fast that I cannot recall
That I was mad or sad at all.
A little bit of fool in me
Keeps evergreen my inmost tree.

(ca. 1963)   *1964*

Sadface at Five

How came sorrow to his eye?
On the one-winged butterfly
At orange half-mast on the twig?
In the black cat's grassy dig
And jungle knack that snatched the bird
Down from the limb? (No moan,
      no word for crippled notes:
      his leg alone
      felt knuckled denim
      at the bone.)

Or in the twist of traitor belt
That whipped his lie, his martyr's welt,
The path he gave his friend to cross?
Who took that baby boy? Whose loss
will hug the pause in his embrace
And nurse the musing in his face
So gravely alive?
Oh, Sadface at five.

(ca. 1964)   *1964*

28

Challenge, Taken Hard

Some beast has pawed the ground,
Some horn-tossed, angry slap of sound
Like mud has stained my brow.
A nostrilled creature, rigid now,
Half chosen, chooses me. A thrill
Of manliness, a shock of will
Fits tightly as a coat of mail,
And I, half tossed, full heaped in a wail
Far-minded, dim, so fiercely choose
That garments stretch and sinews fuse
And breathing joins the rips of sound
That snatch all brisk fears underground.
Some trampling rhythm shakes the air,
And we high-shouldered, intense pair,
Primeval as from switching rain,
Sleeping dust and knocking pain,
Are amphitheatred, straight met,
Hard locked in struggling silhouette.
Some beast has pawed the ground,
Double horned and double frowned.
And we are steeled in strange condition:
One thrill, one snarl of recognition.

(ca. 1964)   *1965*

To a Negro Preacher

Lightning grows old,
Red-ribboned in a luminous page,
Hung down in rage
Rehearsed and kindly sold.
And thunder trickles into song
The pew-line hums along.

Long years of tambourines
Have shaken out unburied cries,
And plates of weary-knuckled coins
Have pyramided to the skies
One callous-handed prayer:
Oh, stricken Christ, be there!

Unhook us, Old Man.
Relax this page before our eyes.
This holy word will keep, will rise
Upon our shoulders African
Before the beast, before the spear.
The jungle test is here.

The benediction of your heart,
The strong brown of your hand
We claim for banners as we start
The Golgotha to free our land.
Help man us on the streets of clay:
We demonstrate today.

(ca. 1964)   *1965*

30

Snowman

I watched him watch
His snowman falling down:
No collapse, no breaking parts,
Nothing to grapple with and hold.
Just smooth, small vanishing
And leaning in the sun.

He watched the carrot nose and finger-fashioned mouth
Turn bump and scar in whining air.
But when the sweat-dark brim of straw
And charcoal eyes
Converged on the tilted pipe,
He shoved, to end his man undone.

I watched the gathering in his face
As he kicked snowy trash,
Growled engine sounds, plowed ditches
Rugged as his will on thawing grass.
But his pity it was not: my whim collapsed, broke up,
With trampled pipe and hat,
And sudden snowball whizzing by.

(ca. 1964)   *1965*

A Poet Does Not Choose to Run

A poet does not choose to run.
His prior nomination
Cannot be undone,
Unwound around the middle
Of his evening self,
His riddle.

What day is this?
He does not count your way,
Hold to your artifice
Of dates and computed men.
He sits uncalendared,
Puzzled thin.

A poet is not yours.
Locked out, locked in,
He opens doors
But cannot stay
To speak for long
Or sit at bay

Unless — and this is strange —
He sits in silence,
His pledge to rearrange
The clues of some wild track,
Trail it lonely out,
And lone come back.

1966   *1966*

32

In Black Suburbia

The worker paused inside the hall,
His quick glance swelling from wall to wall
While he unclipped his scrolls, dark spools
Of signatures to rearrange the schools,
The starting blocks for a race designed
To be fair begun and run abreast
As far as twinborn strength of mind
And equal stretch of will contest.

Did CORE's, did NAACP's desires —
Whatever nerved his aspiration —
See clear the sullen, scattered fires
Tensed in the rug? the twisted aggravation
Of old tissue too deep to die, too scarred to live,
New comfort hard to keep and hard to give
Sidelong in masks of Africa firm on the wall?
(To sign or not to sign . . .) and Is that all?

Outside, the worker closed the whitish gate.
And still it swings, it swings some fate,
Some vastly moving legend to and fro.
Tremblings dim with music come and go.
Brothers on the street have gathered long.
Who sings? Who made that freedom song?

1966   *1966*

33

Taps

Tight sleeve of song,
Raised shoulder high,
Long, numb salute
Far spears the sky.

Unravelled wail
Of smartshot air,
Long furl of hush,
Unquiet stare,
Quick glide of mile,
Lean stretch of dare,
Lightfoot climb
Of steely prayer . . .

Ancestral cry
In captive ear
Upstreaming cold,
But flying clear.

(ca. 1966)   *1967*

Cremation

"Burn him? Burn him up?"
His gasp was only eight.
Our rear-view mirror flowed
to huddled ashes in his eyes
that smarted, quick with sullen flame
that pained the black row of our backs.

The traffic knew. It let him pass
among us, his days of game and riot
clenched like traitors in his fists.
We sat hard and old, but kindly,
in our grief tight as narrowed flag
that rode ahead crisscrossed in bloom.

Downshouldered by his heavy kin,
he swelled, but held his course
with us who could decree
his father useless, think of pit and can.
But we, half-cindered,
leaned into the years,
sifting with love that ample dust.

(ca. 1967)   *[no attempt to publish]*

35

Son

Cross-legged on his bed,
The President is twelve,
Signalling to order all his crew:
Himself as Treasurer, Chief Spy,
Keeper of the Chemicals,
And only member, too.

The minutes of Club Fantastic tell it all:
The Indianheads his paper route turned up for dues,
The four-way-grid code messages he found in shoes,
The fingerprints and buttons marked in basement hush,
The friends he filed away in "Sent by Thrush."

Barefoot at the desk no one disturbs,
The President nods over geometry and German verbs
And Orwell's *1984*, all done.
What can a President do —
Or Treasurer, Chief Spy, Keeper of the Chemicals too —
When all of his fantastic crew,
Despite all signals, doze as one?

Founder of the Club, mystery of twelve,
How signal to you? How softly delve
Into your lonely sleep, that even there, even you
Might close hands with this crew?

(ca. 1966)   *1967*

A Cabinet of Few Affections

The mirror slipped,
And I was gone.
The lather shriveled to an itch,
The incoherent razor sagged,
The sinking path of jaw
Dropped out of sight,
And sight itself
Was senselessly bereft,
Askew, and lurching down
Sharp cheeks of iodine,
A corner bone of talc,
Grey lungs of gauze
That, breathing once, collapsed
Into a mournful box
Below a teethlike row of pills.

To die, to disappear,
And not to be:
These three
Lay quietly
Behind that staring glass
Unhinged.

(ca. 1966)   *1967*

Prayer for a Bigot

Let him have peace: some clanking creed to hail,
Some pinching stools to seat his colic band;
Give him aborted, skulking notes to mail,
Some pseudonyms to libel in the sand.
Toss him some paper beauty to deface,
Plump effigies for plunge of hidden pin;
And for the banner of his hungry race
Some gaudy rag to sew his features in.
But let his anger scrub a lovely cause
Until its sides are bright with truth reclaimed,
And let his keyhole wit grow noisy jaws
As long as fair-beamed halls are uninflamed.
Once let him turn a strong man from his gate,
And turn again, and learn the cost of hate.

(ca. 1967)   *[no attempt to publish]*

For Sousa Junior High, 1967

January bore those rhymes
You christened, questioned new, sprinkling warm
The features of their folded being,
A take-home gift for future times . . .
Programmed, machined, will you again perform
That act of love, the world unseeing?

What girlish eye will dream in wrinkled night;
Will gleam, after years of Readi-Pak,
Pop-Open lunch and Zip-Off can;
Will liquefy old lines that once did fright
And shake the pulse? Will joy spill back
On pain pre-shrunk for man?

Rough astronaut, soft-booted boy,
Push-button walker on the moon,
Odysseus of the long, long bow —
Your sights set on some crystal toy
We now name city, log-in a rhyme with "June"
If laser beams of love dissolve your blow.

1967   *1967*

The Kitchen Phone

Just by taking this phone call
You've won our Bargain Bandit Shawl
Good for discounts until Friday
If worn here with a bonafide
Extra premium go-go purse
You win if you can pronounce in reverse
The letters in this special word
That do-now shoppers have lately heard
TV-wise in our smash campaign
To put you out front. Now, once again:
Five seconds! You have no time to spare.
Hello! Then is your mommy there?

1967   *1967*

The Burlesque Queen

Shook it down
Like lace stepped out of,
Climbed on hesitations
Bunching high,
And floating floating fell.

Quickie globes of breath
Flung up twin fringes
Filling, swinging
Rounding rhythms
Melting winding springs.

Slowdown was a tease
Of circle generating circles
Fluttering again to one,
Running wingward like a ribbon,
Covering none.

(ca. 1968)   *1968*

Lovers, Do Not Think of This

Though you have had your lovers' bliss,
Think not of this:
Not eyes alone
Turn mannikin and slip aside,
Nor lips at last draw quirky lines,
Nor magic brows
Rub out their signs,
Nor kitten fingers
Fold alert designs.

Whole shoulders turn, and go.
Long sinew pulls the bone,
And all the pillowed grasp we have
Uncurls against a stone.
The speechless room is plundered whole,
The blessed tenant fled;
A phrase floats gasping in the swell
Of memory round something said.
Outside, the gate is down, the hinges torn
And stiffly pointed out
At traffic sudden born
And past. It lingers, though —
Strange boulevard —
Some mighty piece of us
To swallow hard.
Like wind, like wind we go.

(ca. 1968)   *1968*

42

Church Burning: Mississippi

In fragrant Dixie's arms
Christ came down in flames,
A smoke-smile on His lips
And black of face
Before the furtive, nail-pierced can
And upthrust beam
Broke charcoal thorns
Across His brow.

The gloried ashes rose
And crossed the heart of Him
Evicted from the land,
Unfisted King whose love was fire enough
To forge the ages,
Martyred Lord, his circling men now weaponed
Only in their eyes.

Some muttered aging prophecies,
Denim pockets bulging knuckles.
Wonder, vague as smoke, if Christ had bled before
He really died
Took some, like coughing, by the throat.
Some rooted young ones broke from Dixie's arms
And dropped like firebrands on the fragrant hearth.

1967   *1970*

43

Fourteen

Something is breaking loose,
    leapfrog-straddling kitchen chair,
    slamdown-toss-up at the mouth,
    joke-dropping sloshings
    stepped on, smeared
    with shoelace dragging
    grinning to himself at

Something almost free and hugging;
    unbroken doors agape behind him
    gasp, and bannisters are lurching
    bending up the stairsteps three-in-one
    he skims, punching a grab of cake
    through jacket sleeve and out again
    caught in his snatched-up cap
    and bounding down again, doors
    standing back.

Upstart train of him is loading,
    whistle-steaming,
    squirting clouds,
    taking precious attic rubbish,
    basement-cornered leaning things . . .

You bundle on a stick
    sneakering by,
    unbroken punch of cake,
    where do you think — oh, think —
    you are going?

1969   *1970*

A Poem for Sarah's Tears

When Sarah fell down in the park,
the birds refused to sing,
the wrens flew silent in the sky,
a sparrow dipped its wing
into a shallow little pool
and wouldn't say a thing.
The flowers acted very strange:
the roses didn't try
to move their thorns to ease the path,
and tree leaves seemed to sigh
while falling yellow through the air
as if to catch the opening eye
and ear of every flower
to help it tell that little girl
"I will not bloom this hour
nor show my pretty face again
until you use my power
to laugh and run through all Kenwood
and smile to all you meet,
'My name is happy Sarah Dawson,
and I live far down the street.' "

1978   *1983*

A Poem for Claire of London

Everyone who knows this girl
or sees her summer face
will bet his pence and pennies too
that she will win her race
to end up on a shining stage
with microphones and bands
and orange and yellow twirling lights
that make the drummer's hands
look autumn magic as he beats
and flatters his twin drums,
while mellow, high-swung beams look down
upon bright Claire, who hums
and moves her shoulders slow
into the rhythm of her song,
while people in the audience
who have been waiting long
are sitting halfway out of their chairs
with hands upon their lips
and hearts as tight as rubber bands
and tingling fingertips
until their pretty Claire swings out
in disco-bistro style
or whatever then the rage might be
to stun the folks a while
and give them what they came to hear:
a famous singer sing,
that girl who ripples every heart
with her own special sting.

1978   *1983*

Scarecrow: the Road to Toulouse

A man, hanging stiffly from the roadside tree,
smeared my eyes awake with sunlight dyes,
and after-luncheon calm burst against the rolling scream
our tires must have sucked into the road,
twisting out of sight that dangling arm.

"What's the French word for *scarecrow*?"
looped out of me like rope to cling to.
She steadied it with words, drove slower
till she saw I understood "Some farmers over here
(not like America, I guess?)
put them in trees. They get in cherry trees" —
the birds, she meant — "and *chuk-chuk-chuk*:
all you get is holes."

I felt the cutting of the beak. The man's head
was gone, back there in the leaves, the limbs,
I hadn't caught it. The other arm, yes,
its tendons of straw crimped, clenched for his signature:
        his bled-out warning
        from the tinsel-threaded legs,
        the ravaged vest,
        the odor-flapping space
        below the bludgeoned, splotchy hat,
        above the splintered broomstick-neck
        (oh, how imagination spun around it,
        scouring hopelessly to raise a human face!) —
        his personal X, a zigzag spasm final, enforceable
        (both law and surname pointing straight to wilderness
        where family of cutlass, musketry, or cannonball
        had blazed his legacy
        through smoking tents and charring huts
        while wild-bird witnesses chanted chaos in the trees).

"Ever wish you were a bird?" she asked,
and roadbed screams carved from me "Right now!
so I could *chuk-chuk-chuk*
against your head and foot to slow us down."
My foot loosened, scraped the floorboard

as if stirring leaves to find some hidden thing.

"If I were a bird," I said,
"I'd know half of everything."
Her discretion let me recalculate, ride a while
with them who fly the land, the grass,
who know all root and leaf and bark, alive and dead.
The scarecrow back there: part of the half
they did not know? Much flesh they know
(the chipmunk's twittery nose, the hippo thrashing),
and little in the seas they think is strange.

Birds know history —
a thought to keep me flying; wherever trees have stood
birds exchanged interpretations,
cancelled out with a *chuk-chuk-chuk* simple facts
(names of events below, above),
negotiating holes (like signs, intentions, signatures),
their perfect eyes remembering the scattered scarecrows
left by cannonball, musketry, and cutlass;
the special Black ones hanging from the trees,
mangled by the personal X of Dixie
(the one receding back there was not Black?
the birds would know).

We know the ritual:
        the hunger-chants expanding trees,
        the downward flutterswoops,
        the legacies free seeded in the field picked up,
        the guardian private breeze aroused,
        swollen to a danger-wind,
        DEATH! sensed and seized,
        the only word the scarecrow-men obey:

        they move grotesquely,
        and from their slightest flap of tinsel,
        drift of odor,
        the air is filled
        with chaos.

1980   *1983*

The Death of Such a One

"It could have been on my face," she said,
and drove with a clash of gears toward the town,
while I, to reconstruct his death,
backed up the mountain, in my mind, right to the spot:
THERE he might have struck,
on the highest hump of road,
black-crusted horseshoe bend, damp and screaming
with the tires she braked and twisted,
her shoulders straining leftward at the turn;
THERE he might have plunged his thin blade home
and sent the car, the driver, back-seat man and me,
with his unthinking self, hurtling,
whirling down to jagged death.

Instead, he'd thrust his needle blow
ten minutes late and stung her off the towntame road
to bump some rusty welcome sign half fallen;
the car had trembled with our jabs and stomps to kill him,
hers and mine, silenced by the back-seat man's reminder:
"This kind," he said, "they leave their sting, then die."

My mind, rescued a second time,
sped down the mountain curves
and caught my hand rolling the window down
to unfist in the swiftborn air
that leaped to whip away his corpse —
one pinch of wing stuck to a torso-smearspot from the floor —
elsewhere his one short spear, bristle-thin
(plucked fast by the back-seat man),
awesome with versions of its past
that scaled the rising window glass
and outmaneuvered every voice we carried,
sound we overtook and passed.

"I hate those things," she said,
speeding up as I slowed down to wonder:
the death of such a one, what did it mean?
A race of unloved creatures, one fearsome sting
apportioned each for his life, his mission, and his curse;
a clan with a brotherhood of almost look-alikes

harnessed by their task to serve us,
sweeten our body needs,
candy some thievish little fingers.
"They're all the same to me," she would think
if the back-seat man or I said "Some make honey";
she would not choose between them,
black or nonblack, mad or tame;
would make her steering wheel, instead,
pretend, swerve us a sharp reminder.

Each choice, it came to me, has only one dimension:
its height or length or width
thinks only how to spend or end a life.
The death of such a one, wingspot snatched from my hand,
was choice enough to pitch again the mountain's height,
the puny width of the slouching post,
between them buzzing drowsily a length of past and purpose
awakening, gathering, poising for its fate —
a ritual tap that might have pierced us to the core.
"It's time to eat," she said, our nods agreeing
to eyesweeps of the street, a search, a choice,
thinking how to spend what kind of noon
to smooth her frowns at her ankle,
her face reassured in the rear-view mirror.

I drifted from their tabletalk, alive
to new dimensions in each sip of wine,
angles, diagonal impressions in each bite of steak,
a swath of aftertaste from spellings on the menu,
a stiff white glove reposing as a napkin,
a lacy hem of apron brushing my hand
when the bill was paid —
my quick fingering so fine
it might have touched, instead,
a memory of wind, of something
not quite in my grasp
chosen to renew itself,
rough up my fabric
with its wing.

1981   *1983*

50

Accident, from a Wajda Movie

Just before he fell into it,
just before the biting gears
and rolling jaws flashed up,
his overseer boots were stomping the old man's groin,
bashing the ribs of the sprawling father
whose Polish tremblings shook out words like "beast"
to face the rapist of his factory daughter,
his thinface jewel, uncased,
the price of her fouled machine,
some cotton cloth unmade:

cotton picked, perhaps, beyond the seas,
by Black slaves branded, flogged,
whipmarched through a maze of overseers
to keep the kingcraft white,
the fiber clean and priceable,
exportable as far as Lódź,
where overseers as grim as Polish fog and dust
made smokestack whistles in the dawn their kindest words,
made warp and woof, unbloodied bolt, their vow
across a hundred flagging necks that dared not turn,
not waver from the monster magnets —
the machines — rattling their iron jaws,
sucking their bladed teeth.

He must have tried to scream,
his overseer boots disappearing,
behind them a lumpy gasp, a slobbering sound
like a mountain giant waking up,
raking one treetrunk arm across his stubbly lips.

The machine stopped, its aftergulp of silence
pulling the old man up, his incredible fingers
still fierce on the enemy's sleeve;
its afterclap of crazed reminders
reddening the cotton cloth;
all witnesses concealed behind two hundred eyes
bloodbound to remember,
but reading in the metal heat new threats,
cruel announcements, foreshadowed
in the sudden whistle blasts,
the running feet, the bosses
stomping in.

1981   *1983*

51

Marijuana Ha-Ha: A Real Smart Dog

U.S. Navy flatfoot, sniffer-outer:
pinch or pound, marijuana's found,
is end of the beeline, on ship or ashore,
when the bluejacket shepherd, the coldnose ace,
is on the case.

Marijuana ha-ha!
Imagine a big-game dog, black,
incorruptible from the nose up,
a single-scent hunter:
RACISM the training rag they filthy soaked and soused,
dripdangled for his puppylore,
wrung out into his growing dome and haunch and withers
for howlfire, for sic-'em strength,
until his muzzle, spine, and tail
forged one straight arrow ready-aimed,
himself like a crouching archer, waiting for the word.

Worthy of him the wilds, the woods
of a New York courtroom, his target hiding there.
Unleash him; somebody dare it,
see him leaping through the necktied, well-washed crowd,
whining here and there at tempting odors
but lunging to approach the bar, the Bench,
white picket fence around the patio of justice
shuddering at his blackness slapping its gate,
his hot sniffs loosening one lawyer's slippers,
shifting her wig on the talking side.

His sleuthing unappeased, hear him frantic,
the Judge's hard-eyed henchman backing off,
the whiffing now a bellows at His Honor's robes,
blasting them up, blowing them down,
snuffing, gulping, swallowing.

Not even surprise
would be left:
just His Honor's empty robes,
settling.

1981   *1983*

52

Sooner or Later, a Close-up

His face filled up the TV screen
to tell our eyes (the camera was thinking)
a problem in shooting films: "Sooner or later,"
his eyebrows helped to say, "you need a close-up,"
and tensions in his lips let us create with him,
"if the face is boring, there is nothing else to see."

A phrase came back to blot out all the rest:
"a face that speaks" — this was the urgency,
the ticket, the usherette, the plush reclining;
but afterthoughts, like stubborn chaff cuffed off the grain,
stuck to some voice unimaged on the screen,
repeating "boring," "boring," "boring,"
demanding that we look at one another,
even if from quiet corners of our seeing,
testing fellow-watchers, trading beams and angles
ended in ourselves and on the screen,
the screen that suddenly went dark,
a momentary breakdown blank enough
to flash across the private screen of each of us
our neighbor's curve of cheek, of brow, of lip,
whatever speaking bits of face gleamed last.

The unexpected silence was itself a question:
when hills and ponds of countenance fade out,
what intensity of light, sensitivity of lens,
can catch their lustre coming back,
reface their stretch and furrow, lift and shine,
reword their shifting text, and theme?

"Boring," "boring," "boring":
even in death, some faces dared the word,
while others, living, wore it like a mask,
a social bandage hiding scars and unhealed places
unphotogenic, unrestorable,
except in special dark — the gentleness of distance
that speaks no names for wounds, for weaknesses,
or, darker still, the anonymity of close-ups
as near as lips to lovers kissing,
breathing the chin and cheek, the eye and brow
they cannot see, care nothing for
until they back away for a close-up.

Sooner or later
the question of distance,
or of love.

1981   *1983*   53

"We Shall Overcome": A Smile for the 1960's

To us, it was a lovely song,
beautiful as a spry old Black woman
leaning backward from her Sunday hymnbook with sad eyes;
it had yester-music, echoes in each pause,
soft cotton sounds and whistling cane,
and, to stand us firm against the day,
knots of slave-time memories:
the rasp of whips, the pitch of chains,
and sullen snap of leg-irons.

It was a lovely song,
beautiful as the lard-rubbed legs of a Black girl
skipping to school on a brand new street,
our undertones, as if her company, cresting on a pain,
a shock from dynamite imagined, and sharp debris;
then arm-in-arm more tensely, thinking back
("They wouldn't hurt a child"),
returning together, living the miracle,
the old faith breaking through, testifying
"We shall overcome."

It was a lovely song,
brave as the Black men, the lordly few,
dying like needful fires snuffed out,
dirtied to extinction by the Backlash rag,
the mask of the low assassins.

But the song was beautiful.
To us, every time, it was lovely,
like the uncut pages of a Book of Dreams —
the best of the century —
pushed aside.

1981   *1983*

54

Ski Boots in Storage

The walls so close, a buckle breaking halfway free
was blocked, some neighbor-cardboard-corner
slipping down
without a cry of "Track! Track!"
to show it had the right,
some dusty hump of plastic bag
crowding the brave toe-line so scarred
no basement-buried tool or silly toy
should dare trespass the barest outline
of its champion print upon the snowless floor.

One boot just right, a bit behind the other,
waiting for the muscled push,
the take-off bite into the mountain snow,
the downward slope leaping up,
loosing its white strands of passage
faster, faster, slicing the sunshine,
tuning the air to its highest key,
till suddenly people, buildings,
swing quickly once, then STOP,
their shapes a vapor
standing still.

1981   *1983*

55

Dirty Old Man

Dirty old man,
caressed by curvy fragrances
from a new mail-order catalog,
fondling virgin corners of the midsection,
musing over elastic little hills, receding caves,
not fingering those familiar places
once your territory, turf, and parking space
you left, reclaimed, and took again
whenever greening luck or ripe design
put license in your hand.
Your eyes, the way you turn the page, say so.

Dirty old man, monitoring the summer park,
x-raying bouncy slacks
for possibilities of magic,
spice for a veteran, a close-mouth man —
sitting there auditioning,
tapping fresh notations on the grass,
instead of hitchhiking to the family plot
to test ungraven headstones, work everybody in.

Dirty old man, rocking on both hands,
imagining prizes: every girl a winner,
every ankle, calf, and pretty thigh
worth socksavings in the mattress;
every blouse, lipstick, and shade of brow
worth a rooftop risk, a steeple fall.

Dirty old man, unwilling to die by the countdown,
won't empty all your pockets on the desk,
won't sign the statement, line up in the queue.
Shame on you.

1981   *1983*

Little Old Black Historian
(For John Hope Franklin)

Little old Black historian,
from the start a greybeard, patriarch,
ordained by his sophomore surprises
the day he dog-eared page on page
where Woodson, Rogers, Wesley
stung him upright, would not go back on their shelf,
would not unspike his chair, unchafe his tie,
ungrip his cut imagination:

stirred from sleep by his fingers searching the bedpost,
he sweat like a runaway slave in the dark,
palms hushing the swamp, feeling a treetrunk for moss,
the sign of its freedom side, its north,
the nighttime push-off for Canada —
and his daylight popcorn hideaways dissolved
as the western movies hocus-pocussed,
the crack cavalry rounding the butte
turning suddenly Black as the Fort Riley 10th,
woolly as the Buffalo Soldiers
bugling the war whoops of their forefathers,
Black chieftains of Indian bands —
strangely riding backwards white again,
rounding the butte, Geronimo dead,
fiercer than Oceola, killed under his flag of truce;

stoking up again on Brawley, Embree, Ottley,
adding more men to the fire (Fort Pillow women, children too),
he fathered four — but none to bear his tuneless dream
of body music hanging from the Southern trees,
none to recognize the corpses in his footnotes,
the slashings-out of lesser heroes like parentheses,
canceled to keep the idea slim, marketable downtown —
while daydreams opened windows to his second book
until an anxious kiddie knock and wound-up voice
said, "How long you gonna be in there?";

years climbed the stairs to answer, slowly,
their books his gems dug up,

worked lovingly from lodes
that glittered back to Mali, Timbuktu,
their monographs his golden track
laid like a winding sheet across the chanting wash
of killer ships (suicides swirling under, hand-in-hand),
their essays his sign carved on the oldest tree,
posthumous promises, ghost-children grieving back:
Dean Derricotte and Bessie Smith so needlessly dead,
Robeson stoned in New York, Roland Hayes clubbed in Georgia,
too many stars for remembrance in a sky brought low;

little old Black historian
raising the firmament, flagging:
can't even say "good morning"
without tears in his eyes.

1981   *1983*

Christmas at the Quaker Center (Paris, 1981)

Once upon a Christmastime
sleighbells snowed the sky
and when I slid the covers back
to slip a wonder-why
through windowfrost I wiped away
I couldn't see a thing
except the hushed Nebraska night
and the little flaky ring
a sparrow dug into the snow
to spring himself to flight.

Once upon a Christmastime
I sneaked a sandwich where
old Santa couldn't miss it:
that table was so bare
his bag of toys and reindeer food
would leave him room to spare,
to sit on while he ate and thought
"This boy is really nice.
I'll search among the toys I've brought
and fill his stocking twice."

Years grew long, and years grew hard,
but I can clear my sight
by twisting certain memories
to make it come out right
that I still hope to see again
a lovely-featured time
that stirs beneath my pillow
and wakes my heart to climb
into the sky on Christmas Eve
and listen to those bells
that ring because I do believe
a snowflake sound that tells
about a sleigh that's coming,
that's driving through the air,

with gifts for everyone who's good,
who struggles to be fair.

And now when I see Santa
I grip him with my eyes,
with all my how-about-its,
with all my tell-me-whys;
and if he takes them standing
and if he shakes my hand
I bag another year of them
and try to understand
this load that makes us human,
those gifts on Santa's back,
our bells for one another
that chime our starry track.

1981   *1983*

Daniel in Paris

"Thieves should be burned alive!"
He hurled it flame-like at the door
and the lock that had let them in,
laced it with curses knotted
fierce as choking.

"Not so loud: you'll wake Daniel."
She seemed to warn her fingers
gliding golden from the curls
relaxed unknowing on his father's chair,
her eyes afraid to lift their disbelief
among the secrets of the room,
each private place incredible:
       that middle drawer snatched open,
       that velvet box scraped out,
       those other fragile gifts awry and rude.

"I knew it couldn't last!"
The wrench of it spilled his bourbon,
pouring out "Just ten more days;
I'm GLAD we're going home!" —
emphatic, like a too-tight bandage.
She meanwhile took his sadness to another room,
sent back "My fur coat's here, at least"
uselessly, too low for his New York flight.

But he returned, and landed hard: "DAMN Paris!" —
a jolt for Daniel, ears and eyes rubbed twice
before the weirdness of the room
seemed playground for orange juice and elbows.
His wake-up whine and squirming to the floor
stopped short when "DAMN Paris!"
shook down its iron lid,
this time a darkness from a stranger's voice,
a pain, a cold vibration.

"We woke up Daniel." "So,

put him to bed. At least, HE doesn't know.
Four months in that nursery,
and he never spoke one word of French.
Smart boy — he'd make a good Parisian."

His hand took up some gold from Daniel's hair,
said nothing more,
and left the rest to her whose jewels were gone,
who would add the losses tomorrow.
Daniel, on her shoulder,
did not know.
And yet he timed it right
to say:
"Je t'aime, Papa, je t'aime."

1982   *1983*

The Telephone Mashers

Halfway out of her coat,
she stared at the telephone book,
opened it again to her name.
THEY'RE ALL CRAZY blinked up in neon words,
that voice again pulsating "Wanta make love right now?"
strangely reversible to DON'T-TURN-AROUND!
urgent as a gun barrel consuming her spine.

Her wall clock moved a shadow down its face,
stirred up an older, watchful voice
whose words once more were naked photos, one by one
hung on the line still coiling in her ear.
Right now, did the telephone move?
Out of the corner of her eye, she caught it,
heard that jivey tone repeating
"It's a PARTY, babe, and YOU can come!"
She had slammed down her name off his lips,
had wiped his silly chuckle off her cheek.

The violence came trembling back,
reverberating threats, the last from a furry voice
above a knife imagined,
slashing her coat, pointing its fierce command —
and then the man that made her cry, The Breather,
who said nothing, just breathed across the line
into her very flesh so hard, so deep
it seemed to sweat.

She almost screamed
when her falling coat sleeve
crackled on the paper bag,
and the groceries felt queer in her arms . . .

And then the phone rang.

1982   *1983*

Snowpit in Switzerland

They always played till dark:
puffy little riders
warm inflated yellow, blue, and red,
ballbundles pushing from the trees,
unfolding on their plastic sleds
across stem-tufted mounds of snow
clamped on the precipice
that bore no air to breathe —
beneath it only icy ribs and slippery veins
for sledways down the crater-bowl
the mountain might have snowballed long ago,
burst and buried in the village rim,
its skyward half up high, today some postcard dome
for tourists, and the sun.

They played always till dark,
their glacier halfworld sucking them down
headfirst and screaming,
handing them up again along the crystal grips
their gloves and boots had hugged into its sides.

Spectators peering down
said nothing clearly,
each "Come home now" and "Do you hear?"
unclaimed below, unused as pocket handkerchiefs.
No looking up, no blip of sky,
no warning boundaries of sense
could unsurprise a snow-clogged mouth,
a dripping eye, a slush-washed ear —
each wet amazement private, unsearchable,
a pitworld promise kept.

Till dark always they played,
the last footprint led away protesting;
then Emptiness stood guard, so firm
the village light grew dimmest there,

no voices grave with duty passed,
no traffic dared to go or stay.
After dark, the village backed away,
leaving the sledworld sovereign,
believable but unreportable,
all its nighttime happenings half true,
the slippage of mountains,
ancient little beckonings
erect again
to keep the new men alive.

1982   *1983*

Andrew's Cyclones

At five, a Giant patrolling awesome stones,
he saw the sudden winds
(impossible as murder in his father's eyes)
whip ropes around his grandpa's house,
whirl up and empty it into the sky —
ran home imagining that bony Black man
floating down, unstruggling,
arms folded high, himself whole as the tumbleweeds
and loops of straw crisscrossing him, loosed
from collisions of darkness and day.

When years gave him his father's eyes
he saw again that bony hand, its denim cap
pocketed with an "Evenin', folks,"
sat on in their front porch swing
and rocked with "That's the way it was in Kansas too" —
the very next day, his voice as cool
as lemonade he took with thankful innocence
and sipped from what he'd learned of cyclones,
his second taste upright and full: "Homesteaders we was,
headin' West to get that lan' an' prove it up,
OWN it" — he smacked his lips to register the deed.

"Them winds was BAD, an' ain' no dus' now
like they was THEN." The swing paused to agree.
"Us Black fam'lies lived in CAVES, you know.
YOU remembers that" — his glass tipped toward his son
and circled back to Andrew, who half rose.
"You could ask Reveren' Mance,
an' ol' 'Pap' Singleton, an' Speese an' 'Manuel,
if they was 'live." The empty glass
almost raised a gesture matching Andrew's,
but the wrinkled cap came up instead
as if to untuck from its folds a stand-up thought:
"THEM was the days — an' they ain' over YET."

"Like Grandpa used to say" lived on
as Andrew's phrase for wading in or swimming out;
his father's face he kept for solid ground, for silence;
rekindled both in midday darknesses:
seasons underground when US BLACK FAM'LIES
(the words dug deeper in) "live in caves,"
low-pressure places,

footings for innocence of breeze —
where cyclones waiting suck it up,
spin chances doors left open take.

His door was closed, but whirlwind-messengers
found magnitudes of path, burst needful air
into his inmost room,
circling news of Southern storms, of islands rocking,
of bushes rattling like spears.
Through him the system gathered, breathed,
pulsed its diameter to ancient grass,
to prairie caves,
to private sky of tumbleweeds and straw,
till "Cyclone 82" they called her,
Killer of the Year.

Now Andrew has grown lean,
studies oath and siege and grappling iron,
looks calm:
arms folded high, as if for floating —
his longitude
and latitude
unreadable, unmistakable
in his eyes.

1982   *1983*

A Bench to Bear

I weigh you on this truth:
a judge will lie,
underneath his robes
a glut of breathing,
not even bloodier around his heart,
not one hair upright on his wrist
that whitens in his darker sleeve,
creeps through, drains out his signature.

Try to believe this heaviness,
this lurch of scale fixed low,
set hard against your ounce:
your little nothing-but-the-truth-
so-help-you-God
so massless, poundless,
small counterweight to perch with
if they catch you Black
or threadbare in your young white coat
or crystal-pillared underneath your reaching.

Believe me: a judge will lie,
will black the Bench with reasons
AMEN'd before, and now, and till the time
assocracies that sit in planetary judgment
are rhythmed with our flesh, with us
who bloody from breathing, from stretching,
from dangling on wrong reasons.

This heaviness will weigh you down
who listen innocent.
Be guilty of this truth;
go thin-clad, stand fragile,
and if they judge you Black,
be crystal.
Shine, shine on them
blinded in their breathing.

1982   *1983*

For Fernand Lagarde (died 13 April 1982)

He was radius abundant,
sweeping our sphere with care,
was diameter keeping us whole,
was promise unstinting,
promptness and the bell.

Though flesh will veer,
remembrance change its tune,
a death intensifies some life,
and one of us, or more,
will sturdy purpose make of him:
our gifts brought through.

Give us this man again
somehow.
We were his only passengers,
his way.

1982 _ *1983*

Note: *Fernand Lagarde was Dean of Liberal Arts, University of Toulouse in France; he died in an auto accident.*

Her Diary

"I'll tell Mr. D. about it,"
she'd say, to send us on our way,
unclarify a private thrill,
unshare a thinwalled pain.
At home, she'd ink it in
while Mr. D., handsome in her need,
waited sail and shore.

"He's beautiful," she thought,
and years improved him
though wrinkles doubled on his face,
grime found little ways to stay,
and words once compliments hung falsely on him,
until the day she cried "Oh, Mr. D.!"
and fled into his room
with more than she could tell,
found him reclining, overfull, as if asleep.

His last phrase she recalled
as flavor of her yesterday
awake and gleaming —
then caught him suddenly about to fall,
his shelf and table stirred
by her brimming;
she found him in her arms,
a first-time feeling:
her Mr. D. a fullness gone,
or realized, an episode complete.

She put him down tenderly,
this girl,
her beauty beginning.

1982   *1983*

Bandages

These ministers amaze,
take their brotherhood into recesses
leanest pilgrims would not try;
never come back alive.

Their robes, perfumeless, pallid,
gather nights untold,
give up their reddened charity unseen,
go thankless to oblivion.

They have no song, no prayer,
require no audience but one,
and him ignore:
his clench of little tears and quiverings
they have no tune for,
bring only vigil, self to share;
and if his hurt is deep and long,
they use no ritual.

Their lives so short, so full
they cannot tend the hurts
that wound the world,
that bleed it at the core —
unbandaged,
estranged from miracles.

1982   *1983*

Blood's the Only Secret

Blood's the only secret —
its hidden streams without seasons
except to feature-forth repeatedly
its mystery;
its blue-emerald of outer rivulets
without history
except what spreads unreadably
through undersurface maps they thread
connecting hill to hill, cave to cave,
networks of territories
nameless in flesh.

Blood's the only secret,
its sound and sense unknowable —
they who hear the sound of it
doomed to nightmares
walling them apart,
and they who learn the sense of it
self-citizened,
reclaimed in racelessness.

Earth's a stainful place to be,
by special bloods islanded,
steeped, steeped in their secrets.

1982   *1983*

Jimboy's Ad

A genius, my camera:
sees you exciting, sensual, dynamic
(are you an actress? model?),
makes you what you want to be;
something works, clicks, for everybody —
something way out, high up if you want,
or really low,
will get it, will turn the key,
will open up their hearts and minds to you.

And/or, my rhythmical exercise plan
will shape you up, do it the musical way,
release your tension, encourage circulation,
channel your energies, balance your body —
without sexual stereotyping or dysfunction,
with lunar, solar, and natal charts standing by,
with regression tips and past-life therapy,
with your psyche plumbed and your healing deep,
with more references than you'll want to see.

And/or, arrangements makeable
for posture-check, clothing coordination,
wine-tasting sessions, lessons on the flute;
I will fill your casserole, pack you a refined picnic,
retouch the shabby lining of your still-good coat,
compose a plain frosting message on your chocolate cake,
typewrite your thesis (I have odd-job UNESCO connections),
and teach you Christian reflection, assertiveness,
self-defense even, in a friendly atmosphere —
cuts and blowdries included
when the weather is right, straight from London.

I also do house painting, plastering,
light carpentry, clean and reasonable;
do cheap and quick removals,
long or short, big or small;
do yardwork, on short notice even;

do counseling on Mondays, sometimes later
if the case is urgent.

I do hypnosis, change your habits:
smoking, drinking, giving in to chronic pain;
and if you need Mexican flour tortillas,
or things like that, I'm your man.
Phone Jimboy, 777-1313. I need work.

1982

1983

Crossing the Square, Montparnasse

Pidgeons almost fly into an old man's face
senselessly, unbirdlike in their beggary,
tame as paper cutouts slippery stepped on,
their scrambling up more disarray than flight
when infant shooings fall into the crumbs.

Sullenly watching, a young man lying cold,
unused to hunger and to stone,
draws up his knees to touch his fists
clenched, as on a cane for rising;
a shape close by, pulled upright by his move,
unwrinkles in its jeans a drowsy puppet girl.

Music to wake her breaks across the square:
a long-haired, bearded trumpeter
tilts back his head and cracks the sky
with a silver beam unchanging in its cry.
No pidgeons cross that track, that hungry climb
sprung from his knees pressed close
like April stems unbending.
He blows, a gathering crowd is warmed,
and one-franc pieces tinkle in his cap.

1982   *1983*

The Broken Bowl

When she felt it slipping,
its green-gold splendor soapy in her hands,
the rainbow bubble
swelling from the faucet mouth
burst, spilled a loudness in her pulse
that blacked a space
where eighty years zigzagged far back, returned
in time to give her gasp a suddenness.

"Don't cry" — her mother saying it so long ago,
the broken forehead of the creamy doll
not even caressable.
"Don't cry" — her father pushing her away,
her mother helping, and then the shot,
the barnyard fence poles not even hiding his collapse,
fragments fitting in her ears about the gopher hole
they said he'd stumbled in before they killed him,
before she found it, filled it with the earth.

She had cried, and years had watched her:
breakage many-voiced as premonitions,
second chances, sharp reminders —
all ceremonious, collectors of payments due . . .

Like now: her gasp half bringing back
"Grandma, let me do the dishes" —
the smallest one, who could barely hold this bowl,
who must have heard but couldn't know
its past, its green-gold splendor.
History and bowls, she thought,
perhaps go hand in hand,

and felt the parts give way,
start a ritual in the sink,
their settling proud.

"Grandma, you finished already?"
was just a way of passing through, to play,
the thought diminishing, continuing
that breakage and pride grow old together,
mislay their strength companionably.
Her fingers, drying, wet themselves again:
a hesitation seeming,
a portion of her blinking, turning,
the reach for her glasses.

A towel slowly wiped them all:
fingers, spectacles, and the thought
of some old splendid thing,
now finished,
unbroken
in its time.

1982   *1983*

All's Fair

"Darling, whose hair is this?"
Opening the drapes, he caught the words in his back,
like a small arrow mismanaged,
her bedside intention first a pinprick thing
aimed vaguely while it grew in all dimensions,
its length a thrust outleaping,
pulling through itself her shaft of iron,
fixed where he first felt it.

"I don't know," he yawned,
a masterful effort in his throat,
arms raised as if to face a false arrest.
Her relaxation, engagement with a stocking
had almost brought them down when she continued
"You haven't even looked at it,"
her winner-of-the-round expression
holding steady while he countered
with a truth that turned up presto:
"Could be one of yours,"
his eyes reaching across her for cigarettes.

"It's one of mine, all right" —
this without a second look;
her tone, pleased with its timing,
outlasted his swallow
in giving lift to her "Shall I go first?"
daintily, as if she meant to seed a window box of flowers.

"Why not?"
He said it like two light scars upon the floor
some heavy chair legs would have made,
dragged quickly out of her path;
and soon the bathtub water running
sounded wrong: like a draining out.

1982   *1983*

78

Antonić Gomić (At Monument Park in Yugoslavia)

Little Antonić
is hiding in these walls:
old plaster in his teeth,
red brick in his eyes,
long bodies pressing him —
all must be mortaring his screams.

And yet we hear you, Antonić;
we relive the terror
you were not old enough to feel;
we see your wide-eyed fumblings,
fingerings toward the smiling door
the beast with the bayonet broke through
to leave you massacred,
melted in the courage of your town,
the memory bloodied, steadied,
for us.

Little Antonić,
even then you could not hide:
so small he hardly saw you,
but now grown tall
as all those townsmen dead beside you,
partisans, Antonić, beckoning us,
us, his enemies, Yes!, forever,
his brutal helmet our signal
to plaster, brick, and mortar
all our little strengths together,
to firm that courage yet-to-be,
needed, Antonić, NEEDED,
like the deathless memory
of you.

1982   *1983*

Sis and the Pidgeon Man

I remember the broken bottles,
the lurch to avoid them,
the soft black country earth like foam torn into,
mending instantly on my wheels
not stopped until she jumped out, running,
her one-year-old her armful almost dropped,
awakened by "Here's Sis!" cried out from the porch.

The shouting set the tone, the pace,
her homecoming like a favorite wooden bench —
come loose and set aside the day she went away —
now found and reassembled noisily
for the three of them to sit on
("Sis" to them, her brother and his wife)
jostling one another with old brown wrappings
of jokes remembered, of news retold.

His brusque arm ordered beer,
his quick glance measuring me
like acreage, distance, or the weight of grain —
no detective work to rename the father of the child,
just habit, like squinting at clouds —
his booming handclap soon untightening the air,
signalling our beer cans open, popping,
Sis's infant girl flying upward,
tossed high with his restless laugh,
one syllable to scorn the chance
his arms were taking,
one rhythm in his feet to beat away dissent
until his wife — all olive, lemon, sun-rinsed lime —
found stone enough
to build a little wall around him.

We talked above it while he joked it down,
watched him step across it, break out into business,
pushing us to see his pidgeons (hundreds, he said),
his shitty boots leading us, manly sounding
in their muddy way of making-do,
of sucking up his explanations:
all breadwinning, mastery — calculations
too tricky to follow.

"We unpacked some of your stuff, Sis,
the way you said." He waved us houseward

like a man lingering for grave affairs,
uphill, aloof from trifles, trinkets
in Sis's room, an island, a disbelief
of fragrant, regal clutter,
staggered postures of her pencilled faces,
of water colors foreign, drifting,
their ports of call a crazy quilt of Indian silks,
drowsy curtains, cinnamon masks,
Egyptian beetles, stubborn canes,
and tiny, smoke-hued elephants.

Sis and the pidgeon man:
their lace and burlap somehow from a single cloth —
a fact, a life-perfume
inhalable from filth, from rainbow strands.
Feelings from her skirt came up to me
as momentary rain puffing incense from the dust
just as his new-washed hand and bright-rolled sleeve,
hugging his sister, pulled her outside.

His free arm was for me,
an iron band
bracing the tug of Welcome! Welcome!
sure of the real air,
of soiled wings, and of stone.

1982   *1983*

Françoise and the Fruit Farmer

In town to sell his fruit, he saw her —
Françoise in her summer slacks —
turning to him, coming back
to feel the swelling plums,
one held in each soft hand, breast-high,
above them her eyes enclosing him
in quietness brushed up to colors,
urgings green, thrustings yellow.

A vine-like touch, her promise seemed all profit,
surplus to lay aside and store,
quick harvest if he collapsed his stand,
pulled down his crates, rolled away his canvas;
full bounty if he washed his hands and followed,
trailing her fragrances
of melons in their prime, of berries bursting.

She turned to go, her scent adrift
as if from glistenings in soil turned off a spade.
His yearning had no time
to plant and cultivate
and wait for rain,
yet he was quick to catch a peach about to fall —
that brightness of his wrist
costing the moment that concealed her in the crowd;
and yet a perfect peach lay in his hand,
his only means to feel the way good seasons end.

A lucky day, he thought,
begins with plums.

1982   *1983*

82

Racism in France

"But there's racism in France too."
She said it almost tenderly,
lifting the dessert,
the glazed cherries gleaming on the pie,
its maiden slice for me, the guest.
I nodded, noncommittal, at the second piece,
their blondish daughter reaching for it,
quick, like almost nine years old,
her father's eye a brake that could not hold;
her mother's hand a lesson lost:
in serving him, its careful demonstration
was outmaneuvered in the nearest room
by Jacqueline's favorite TV program,
"Once Upon a Time," her anarchy kept low.

"You must have noticed it."
Her eyebrow-crinkle at the end
censured the excuse-me swallow of Jacqueline,
whose agile disappearance
vaguely re-arranged the odds, the focus.
"Perhaps," I replied, "but . . ."
and I missed Jacqueline's facing me,
the wild geometry of her knife and fork
unquestioned, her cave habitable by common accord.

And we live in rocks hollowed out,
erodable, I thought, vulnerable
when the wind is loaded with a nearby care
half-heavy, like something in that motherly voice
insistent as the cherry pit
that stuck its bit of stone,
suddenly, into the teeth of my answer:

"Imagine Jacqueline."
Their eyes, expecting rigors,
made no adjustment, waited,
friendly targets I had not wanted.
"How would she feel,"
my arrow loosened in its sheaf,
"if she saw you putting poison into her food?"
Their hands flapped up as if to scatter flies,
their pursed lips patient.
"Not real poison, not even real food,

not something to KILL her" —
the barb, if any, their eyes admitted,
could be coming up, taking aim —
"but something to contaminate her tongue,
so that, forever, the taste of home-things
would sicken her, make her remember
you despised her without cause,
planned her destruction."

"But that's unnatural; that couldn't happen";
and TV sounds (their glances sideways said) agreed,
slowed down my arrow in its flight.
The targets held themselves upright,
protectable, until I said
"It happened to me."
They leaned forward as if blown by wind.
"You don't mean that your PARENTS . . .?"
They bent beneath the load imagined
till I halfway restored them,
saying "No, I don't mean that, not them."

My silence filled their eyes with speculation,
their humanness so right, so naively wrong
it could not penetrate the darkness meant,
could only glow at it, like a butterfly
luminescent in fragile balance, stiffening.
"The ones who did it" —
my definition did not grow toward them —
"mean less than Jacqueline, than what you make of her";
they seemed to want to swim the lake of sound
around her, a rescue team.
"That is, imagine her abroad
still in search of love, or less,
meal by meal escaping you — a homeless foreigner,
shedding native smells of scorn and carcass-notions,
her tablemates now shining, palms-up."

Small gestures wiped their honest hands,
patrolled the merchandise they wore, discreetly.
"Imagine her brought home by the stench returning
perhaps perfumed in a friendly question,

or unbarreled publicly, bursting out from shattered glass
or rooftops powdering, smokewhispers coughing up
from a hate-bomb the news of the day."

The vision clanked in iron shoes around them
till I stopped it:
"Jacqueline would read the headlines HER way:
'HOME-GROWN POISON KILLS EIGHT, WOUNDS THIRTY;
FOREIGNERS NOT INVOLVED.' "
I paused. They could not taste it,
could not know,
not feel some family arrow
turning, burning through the night.

We smiled incapabilities
into our genial coffee,
each white cup silent,
dark, and strangely warm.

1982   *1983*